Francis Frith's
NORTH YORKSHIRE

PHOTOGRAPHIC MEMORIES

Francis Frith's
NORTH YORKSHIRE

◆

Clive Hardy

FRITH
BOOK Co

First published in the United Kingdom in 1999 by
Frith Book Company Ltd

Hardback Edition
ISBN 1-85937-048-9

Paperback Edition 2000
ISBN 1-85937-236-8

Paperback Reprinted 2001

British Library Cataloguing in Publication Data

Francis Frith's North Yorkshire
Clive Hardy

Frith Book Company Ltd
Frith's Barn, Teffont,
Salisbury, Wiltshire SP3 5QP
Tel: +44 (0) 1722 716 376
Email: info@francisfrith.co.uk
www.francisfrith.co.uk

Printed and bound in Great Britain

AS WITH ANY HISTORICAL DATABASE THE FRITH ARCHIVE IS CONSTANTLY BEING CORRECTED AND IMPROVED
AND THE PUBLISHERS WOULD WELCOME INFORMATION ON OMISSIONS OR INACCURACIES

CONTENTS

◆

FRANCIS FRITH: *Victorian Pioneer*

FRANCIS FRITH, Victorian founder of the world-famous photographic archive, was a complex and multitudinous man. A devout Quaker and a highly successful Victorian businessman, he was both philosophic by nature and pioneering in outlook.

By 1855 Francis Frith had already established a wholesale grocery business in Liverpool, and sold it for the astonishing sum of £200,000, which is the equivalent today of over £15,000,000. Now a multi-millionaire, he was able to indulge his passion for travel. As a child he had pored over travel books written by early explorers, and his fancy and imagination had been stirred by family holidays to the sublime mountain regions of Wales and Scotland. 'What a land of spirit-stirring and enriching scenes and places!' he had written. He was to return to these scenes of grandeur in later years to 'recapture the thousands of vivid and tender memories', but with a different purpose. Now in his thirties, and captivated by the new science of photography, Frith set out on a series of pioneering journeys to the Nile regions that occupied him from 1856 until 1860.

INTRIGUE AND ADVENTURE

He took with him on his travels a specially-designed wicker carriage that acted as both dark-room and sleeping chamber. These far-flung journeys were packed with intrigue and adventure. In his life story, written when he was sixty-three, Frith tells of being held captive by bandits, and of fighting 'an awful midnight battle to the very point of surrender with a deadly pack of hungry, wild dogs'. Sporting flowing Arab costume, Frith arrived at Akaba by camel seventy years before Lawrence, where he encountered 'desert princes and rival sheikhs, blazing with jewel-hilted swords'.

During these extraordinary adventures he was assiduously exploring the desert regions bordering the Nile and patiently recording the antiquities and peoples with his camera. He was the first photographer to venture beyond the sixth cataract. Africa was still the mysterious 'Dark Continent', and Stanley and Livingstone's historic meeting was a decade into the future. The conditions for picture taking confound belief. He laboured for hours in his wicker dark-room in the sweltering heat of the desert, while the volatile chemicals fizzed dangerously in their trays. Often he was forced to work in remote tombs and caves where conditions were cooler. Back in London he exhibited his photographs and was 'rapturously cheered' by members of the Royal Society. His reputation as a photographer was made overnight. An eminent modern historian has likened their impact on the population of the time to that on our own generation of the first photographs taken on the surface of the moon.

VENTURE OF A LIFE-TIME

Characteristically, Frith quickly spotted the opportunity to create a new business as a specialist publisher of photographs. He lived in an era of immense and sometimes violent change. For the poor in the early part of Victoria's reign work was a drudge and the hours long, and people had precious little free time to enjoy themselves.

Most had no transport other than a cart or gig at their disposal, and had not travelled far beyond the boundaries of their own town or village. However, by the 1870s, the railways had threaded their way across the country, and Bank Holidays and half-day Saturdays had been made obligatory by Act of Parliament. All of a sudden the ordinary working man and his family were able to enjoy days out and see a little more of the world.

With characteristic business acumen, Francis Frith foresaw that these new tourists would enjoy having souvenirs to commemorate their days out. In 1860 he married Mary Ann Rosling and set out with the intention of photographing every city, town and village in Britain. For the next thirty years he travelled the country by train and by pony and trap, producing fine photographs of seaside resorts and beauty spots that were keenly bought by millions of Victorians. These prints were painstakingly pasted into family albums and pored over during the dark nights of winter, rekindling precious memories of summer excursions.

THE RISE OF FRITH & CO

Frith's studio was soon supplying retail shops all over the country. To meet the demand he gathered about him a small team of photographers, and published the work of independent artist-photographers of the calibre of Roger Fenton and Francis Bedford. In order to gain some understanding of the scale of Frith's business one only has to look at the catalogue issued by Frith & Co in 1886: it runs to some 670

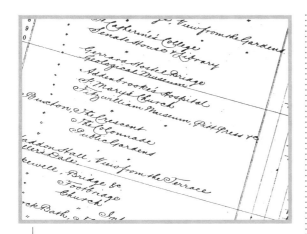

pages, listing not only many thousands of views of the British Isles but also many photographs of most European countries, and China, Japan, the USA and Canada – note the sample page shown above from the hand-written *Frith & Co* ledgers detailing pictures taken. By 1890 Frith had created the greatest specialist photographic publishing company in the world, with over 2,000 outlets – more than the combined number that Boots and WH Smith have today! The picture on the right shows the *Frith & Co* display board at Ingleton in the Yorkshire Dales. Beautifully constructed with mahogany frame and gilt inserts, it could display up to a dozen local scenes.

POSTCARD BONANZA

The ever-popular holiday postcard we know today took many years to develop. In 1870 the Post Office issued the first plain cards, with a pre-printed stamp on one face. In 1894 they allowed other publishers' cards to be sent through the mail with an attached adhesive halfpenny stamp. Demand grew rapidly, and in 1895 a new size of postcard was permitted called the

court card, but there was little room for illustration. In 1899, a year after Frith's death, a new card measuring 5.5 x 3.5 inches became the standard format, but it was not until 1902 that the divided back came into being, with address and message on one face and a full-size illustration on the other. *Frith & Co* were in the vanguard of postcard development, and Frith's sons Eustace and Cyril continued their father's monumental task, expanding the number of views offered to the public and recording more and more places in Britain, as the coasts and countryside were opened up to mass travel.

Francis Frith died in 1898 at his villa in Cannes, his great project still growing. The archive he created continued in business for another seventy years. By 1970 it contained over a third of a million pictures of 7,000 cities, towns and villages. The massive photographic record Frith has left to us stands as a living monument to a special and very remarkable man.

Frith's Archive: *A Unique Legacy*

FRANCIS FRITH'S legacy to us today is of immense significance and value, for the magnificent archive of evocative photographs he created provides a unique record of change in 7,000 cities, towns and villages throughout Britain over a century and more. Frith and his fellow studio photographers revisited locations many times down the years to update their views, compiling for us an enthralling and colourful pageant of British life and character.

We tend to think of Frith's sepia views of Britain as nostalgic, for most of us use them to conjure up memories of places in our own lives with which we have family associations. It often makes us forget that to Francis Frith they were records of daily life as it was actually being lived in the cities, towns and villages of his day. The Victorian age was one of great and often bewildering change for ordinary people, and though the pictures evoke an impression of slower times, life was as busy and hectic as it is today.

We are fortunate that Frith was a photographer of the people, dedicated to recording the minutiae of everyday life. For it is this sheer wealth of visual data, the painstaking chronicle of changes in dress, transport, street layouts, buildings, housing, engineering and landscape that captivates us so much today. His remarkable images offer us a powerful link with the past and with the lives of our ancestors.

TODAY'S TECHNOLOGY

Computers have now made it possible for Frith's many thousands of images to be accessed almost instantly. In the Frith archive today, each photograph is carefully 'digitised' then stored on a CD Rom. Frith archivists can locate a single photograph amongst thousands within seconds. Views can be catalogued and sorted under a variety of categories of place and content to the immediate benefit of researchers. Inexpensive reference prints can be created for them at the touch of a mouse button, and a wide range of books and other printed materials assembled and published for a wider, more general readership - in the next twelve months over a hundred Frith local history titles will be published! The

THE FRANCIS FRITH COLLECTION
Photographic publishers since 1860

HOME | PHOTO SEARCH | BOOKS | PORTFOLIO | GALLERY   MY CART
Products | History | Other Collections | Contact us | Help?

your town,
your village

365,000
photographs of 7,000 towns and villages, taken between 1860 & 1970.

The Frith Archive
The Frith Archive is the remarkable legacy of its energetic and visionary founder. Today, the Frith archive is the only nationally important archive of its kind still in private ownership.

The Collection is world-renowned for the extraordinary quality of its images.

The Gallery
This month The Frith Gallery features images from "Frith's Egypt".

News...
Image update complete.
An additional 5,000 images have been added and the quality of all images has now been improved.

Sample Chapters avaiable.
The first selection of sample chapters from the Frith Book Co.'s extensive range is now available. All are offered in Pdf format for easy downloading and viewing.

explore
FRITH
Search thousands of photographs from one of the worlds' great archives.

Town search

County search
Select a county

the **FRITH**gallery

See Frith at www. francisfrith.co.uk

day-to-day workings of the archive are very different from how they were in Francis Frith's time: imagine the herculean task of sorting through eleven tons of glass negatives as Frith had to do to locate a particular sequence of pictures! Yet the archive still prides itself on maintaining the same high standards of excellence laid down by Francis Frith, including the painstaking cataloguing and indexing of every view.

It is curious to reflect on how the internet now allows researchers in America and elsewhere greater instant access to the archive than Frith himself ever enjoyed. Many thousands of individual views can be called up on screen within seconds on one of the Frith internet sites, enabling people living continents away to revisit the streets of their ancestral home town, or view places in Britain where they have enjoyed holidays. Many overseas researchers welcome the chance to view special theme selections, such as transport, sports, costume and ancient monuments.

We are certain that Francis Frith would have heartily approved of these modern developments, for he himself was always working at the very limits of Victorian photographic technology.

THE VALUE OF THE ARCHIVE TODAY

Because of the benefits brought by the computer, Frith's images are increasingly studied by social historians, by researchers into genealogy and ancestory, by architects, town planners, and by teachers and school-children involved in local history projects. In addition, the archive offers every one of us a unique opportunity to examine the places where we and our families have lived and worked down the years. Immensely successful in Frith's own era, the archive is now, a century and more on, entering a new phase of popularity.

THE PAST IN TUNE WITH THE FUTURE

Historians consider the Francis Frith Collection to be of prime national importance. It is the only archive of its kind remaining in private ownership and has been valued at a million pounds. However, this figure is now rapidly increasing as digital technology enables more and more people around the world to enjoy its benefits.

Francis Frith's archive is now housed in an historic timber barn in the beautiful village of Teffont in Wiltshire. Its founder would not recognize the archive office as it is today. In place of the many thousands of dusty boxes containing glass plate negatives and an all-pervading odour of photographic chemicals, there are now ranks of computer screens. He would be amazed to watch his images travelling round the world at unimaginable speeds through network and internet lines.

The archive's future is both bright and exciting. Francis Frith, with his unshakeable belief in making photographs available to the greatest number of people, would undoubtedly approve of what is being done today with his lifetime's work. His photographs, depicting our shared past, are now bringing pleasure and enlightenment to millions around the world a century and more after his death.

NORTH YORKSHIRE – *An Introduction*

The largest of all the English shires, Yorkshire once comprised an area of 3.75 million acres divided into three ridings; the West Riding was bigger than any other county, and the North Riding came in at a respectable fourth place. Just when the boundaries of Yorkshire were fixed is not known for certain, but its formation along with Nottinghamshire, Leicestershire and Lincolnshire occurred when the area was known as the Danelaw. We do know that the southern boundary of Yorkshire conformed closely to the old border between Northumbria and Mercia. The counties of Southern England are far older, while those of the Midlands and the North appear to date from the tenth and eleventh centuries.

Yorkshire was once a part of the great Saxon kingdom of Northumbria, which at its height reached from the Humber to the Forth. By the 9th century, however, territory was being lost to the Scots, and the country was ravaged by Norse raiders who were searching for gold, plunder and slaves. The Vikings eventually settled throughout much of present-day Yorkshire, and Viking or Norse-Irish kings ruled from York.

In AD910 an offensive was launched from the Danelaw in an all-out attempt to finish off the West Saxons. It went wrong. They were heavily defeated by Edward the Elder, with the help of his sister Elthelfleda, the widow of Earldorman Ethelred of Mercia, who then launched a counter-offensive aimed at the total re-conquest of the Danelaw. Tamworth, Derby and Leicester all fell to Ethelfleda's troops. By AD920 Edward was grudgingly acknowledged as overlord by Northumbria and the Welsh. Under Edward's successor Athelstan, West Saxon control was extended beyond the Tees, and a major defeat was inflicted upon a combined Danish, Welsh, and Scottish army at Brunanburh. After Athelstan died in AD939, Northumbria once again asserted its independence, and it was only after Eric Bloodaxe, the last Viking king of York, died in battle in AD954, that West Saxon control was restored. Even then, it was not strong enough to prevent the Scots from conquering Lothian.

The Battle of Hastings did not hand England to William the Conqueror on a plate. A rising in Kent was suppressed, but by the second half of 1068 anti-Norman feeling in

Yorkshire was so high that William was forced to march north. In 1069 there were two northern-led rebellions, the second of which was by far the most dangerous for William, in that it was supported by a Danish fleet in the Humber. As William approached York, the Danes abandoned the city and fell back on the Isle of Axholme. But if William thought matters would soon be over, he was wrong: the Mercians, aided by Welsh allies, also took to the field. Leaving a force to watch the Danes, William marched on Stafford, where he won an easy victory. By the end of the year he was

waste. Symeon of Durham wrote of William's harrying of the North. He described the devastation wrought on towns, villages and farmsteads, and of the corpses left to rot where they had fallen; Yorkshire was indeed paying a terrible price for defying the Normans.

Yorkshire is blessed with a rich tradition influenced by Anglians, Danes, Flemings, Norwegians, Norse-Irish and even the Normans. The twelfth century chronicler, William of Malmesbury, noted that the Northern English dialect was unintelligible to people from the south; it was also a fact of life

campaigning along the Tees when news of another Mercian revolt reached him. William took his troops across the Pennines into Cheshire, established a castle at Chester, and then moved south to Stafford where another castle was built.

The Conqueror's reprisals during 1069-70 were deliberate and at times savage. They were aimed at crushing resistance once and for all. Almost the whole of the population of north Lancashire was driven out, and over half the villages in the North Riding and one-third in both East and West Ridings were laid

that royal writs had to be translated so that Northerners could understand them.

With the Normans came the founding of the great Cistercian abbeys such as Fountains, Rievaulx, Kirkstall and Jervaulx. Though endowed with lands by Norman lords eager to gain a place in heaven, their ultimate wealth and power lay in the production of wool. Fountains alone would have over 600,000 acres given over to sheep pasture. Much of the wool went for export, but by the early 14th century an embryonic Yorkshire woollen industry existed at York, and later Beverley, and would soon spread to Leeds, Bradford, Huddersfield and Halifax.

Apart from the woollen industries, centred round its abbeys, North Yorkshire lead mining was developed around the Grassington and Pateley Bridge areas. From the early 17th century, alum mines were opened on the coast. In the 13th century, ironmaking was tried in Rosedale, but there were problems in obtaining quality coal. The coal found on the west Moorlands was poor, though adequate for burning lime, and there were logistical problems in transporting coal from mines around Easingwold and Thirsk. Copper was once mined at Middleton Tyas, and it was also discovered in the Richmond area, but it proved uneconomical to extract.

THE AGE OF INDUSTRY

At the beginning of the 19th century, England was still a rural country with less than a third of the population living in towns, and only one in five of those in a town of more than 20,000 inhabitants. In 1811 the total population for Yorkshire was given as 973,113. By the census of 1821 it had risen to 1,173,187. Of these, 799,357 lived in the West Riding, with 190,449 in the East, and 183,381 in the North. By the end of Victoria's reign things had changed, with only one in five people still living in the country. Some of these rises in population have been dramatic. The best known is that of Middlesbrough, which in 1801 had consisted of just four houses and twenty-five people. Things changed, however, when Middlesbrough was chosen by the Stockton & Darlington Railway as the site for a number of staithes, where coal could be trans-shipped for delivery by sea. Joseph Pease was responsible not only for extending the railway to Middlesbrough but also for laying out the new town which consisted of a dozen or so streets of houses, a market square, town hall, and a parish church. By 1841 the population had rocketed to 5,463 inhabitants; the staithes were moving around 1.5 million tons of coal a year, and additional industries had already sprung up in the form of a pottery, foundry and a rolling mill. Henry Bolckow

opened an iron works in 1841, in partnership with John Vaughan who already had iron working experience. At first they depended on imported ore, but from the 1850s local ore from the Cleveland Hills became available. By 1873 Teesside was producing about one-third of the entire British output of iron, local ore meeting 84 per cent of the requirement. In less than one hundred years Middlesbrough had grown from an obscure hamlet to a large industrial town of 91,000 people.

Some towns grew at a faster rate than others. By 1851 York was no longer the great northern city of old, but had been overtaken by Leeds, Sheffield, Bradford and Hull. With the rise of Middlesbrough, so came North Yorkshire's involvement in shipbuilding on a grand scale. True, building had gone on for years at places like Whitby; but the ironmaking along the Tees, readily available supplies of coal and coke, a massive influx of people wanting work, and shipowners needing steamships came together to produce an industry to rival that on the Wear and the Tyne. Rake, Kimber & Co opened a shipyard on the Tees in 1858, on a site now occupied by the transporter bridge. They built the 'De Brus', the first iron ship to be built at Middlesbrough, but after completing only three more vessels the yard closed owing to lack of orders. It was taken over by Richardson, Duck & Co who already had a yard at Stockton, and it was they who put a young man by the name of Raylton Dixon in charge. By 1873 Raylton had secured the yard for himself and renamed it Raylton Dixon & Co; his first ship was the 2,099 iron steamer 'Torrington' for the Commercial Steam Shipping Co. The yard went on to build ships for some of the great shipping companies of the late 19th and early 20th centuries, including Lamport & Holt, Elder Dempster, Hansa Line of Hamburg, Bergen Line, Wilson Line of Hull, and Houlder Line. Other ship yards on the Yorkshire side of the Tees were Smith's Dock at South Bank, and Robert Craggs & Co, which opened on land adjacent to Sir Raylton Dixon's yard.

SPA TOWNS AND BATHING PLACES

At just under 21 miles from Whitby, Scarborough rapidly developed to become the premier resort on the Yorkshire coast. It was a spa town; its waters were discovered by a certain Mrs Farrow around 1626. The earliest building over the spa was little more than a wooden shelter built for the convenience of people drinking the waters. Disaster struck in 1737 when a landslide destroyed the spa, and it was two years before it could be reopened. By this time, the spa was housed in a pump room, but this too was destroyed and replaced in 1839.

Scarborough was now a major tourist attraction for the genteel classes, and this was reflected in the new buildings, which by the late 1850s included a concert hall. Scarborough continued to maintain its genteel airs and graces, and objected to the coming of the railway, on the grounds that it wanted nothing to do with the lower social orders. 'The watering place has no wish for a greater influx of vagrants, and those who have no money to spend.' Be that as it may, Scarborough did become popular with working people, though for a number of years it managed to maintain two distinct seasons, a fashionable one and a popular one.

At one time Scarborough was the only harbour between the Humber and the Tees where ships of a large burden could run for cover from North Sea storms. During the reign of George II, a duty was levied on all coal loaded on the Tyne, in order to pay for Scarborough's pier, which was extended to a length of 1,200ft. Facilities were further improved with the construction of a second pier of 1,300ft using stone quarried from White Nabb. By 1820 the harbour was handling around 25,000 tons of cargo a year. Exports were mainly corn, butter, hams, bacon and salted fish; imports included coal from Newcastle, timber from the Baltic, and wines and spirits from France and the Netherlands.

Harrogate is one of the oldest and most loved of the English spa towns. Its curative

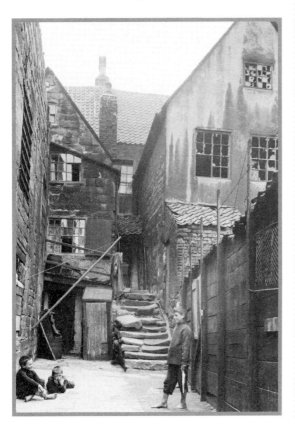

mineral springs were discovered by Sir William Slingsby in 1571. Slingsby's discovery was different, in that it was the first spring not connected with the holy wells of old. In Slingsby's day, the town of Harrogate did not exist.

The area was moorland within the Royal Forest of Knaresborough. By the middle of the 17th century the sulphur well was in use; when the naturalist John Ray visited it in 1661, he wrote that 'though it be pellucid enough, yet it stinks noisomely, like rotten eggs'. The town was developed as a spa in the 1840s by the Duchy of Lancaster. The first public baths opened in 1842.

By 1906 it was being described as having a 'high and bracing situation among the Yorkshire moors, and ranks with Bath and Buxton among the three chief inland watering places of England. It consists of two parts, High and Low Harrogate, the former to the left of the station, the latter to the right. It is perhaps the most aristocratic of all the great English spas'. The sulphur springs, of which there were two that were strong and seventeen that were mild, were said to be efficacious 'for most affectations of the liver, jaundice, gout, rheumatism, and diseases of the skin. The six chalybeate springs are tonic and stimulant. The so-called bog-springs, of which there are 34 in number, rise in a small piece of boggy ground a little to the West of the sulphur-springs, and though close together no two are exactly alike'. When 'taking the waters' fell out of fashion, Harrogate did not roll over and die like Buxton. Astute marketing and a sense of purpose saw the town develop into the premier conference centre in the country.

MIDDLESBROUGH, THE MARKET PLACE 1913 66408

On the left is the old Town Hall, which was built in 1846; the town fire engine was also kept here. A new and rather grand Town Hall, designed by Alfred Waterhouse, was opened in 1889 by the Prince of Wales; it cost £130,000 to build.

MIDDLESBROUGH, CORPORATION ROAD 1901 47979

The electric street tramway system operated on 3ft 6in gauged track, and opened in 1898, the same year as similar systems in Bradford, Glasgow, Halifax, Liverpool, Stockton, Cork and Kidderminster.

MIDDLESBROUGH
Linthorpe Road 1913 66411
Linthorpe Road was at one time the town's only road south. Originally, development along here had been for residential purposes, but as early as the 1860s some of the houses were being converted into retail premises. By the end of the 1870s it had become one of the principal shopping areas.

MIDDLESBROUGH, THE OPERA HOUSE 1913 66405
The Grand Opera House opened in 1904 at a cost of £38,000, but struggled and was taken over by John Imeson in 1909. Imeson was one of the leading figures in the town's entertainment business; his involvement with the theatre began in 1866, when he started building the Royal Albert Theatre. In 1870 it was renamed the Theatre Royal and did extremely well, presenting a wide variety of shows ranging from comedies to pantomimes and operas.

MIDDLESBROUGH, THE TRANSPORTER BRIDGE 1913 66412
Before the commissioning of the transporter bridge a ferry operated across the Tees to Port Clarence. The transporter bridge was designed and built by the Cleveland Bridge & Engineering Co and was opened for traffic in 1911. It is the largest of its type in the world, at 850ft long and 215ft high.

MIDDLESBROUGH, THE PARK 1913 66413
Albert Park was opened by Prince Arthur, Duke of Connaught, in 1868, and the land was purchased for the town
by Henry Bolckow. The park was the scene of a spectacular firework display in 1881, held to celebrate the town's
jubilee.

REDCAR, FROM THE PIER 1896 37593

The population in 1801 was 431, but this had dropped to 411 by the time of the 1811 census. The census return for 1821 caused a minor sensation when it was discovered that the men were outnumbered by 3 to 2: there were 279 males and 394 females.

REDCAR, THE PIER 1896 37594

Though popular, Redcar suffered for years, along with other Teesside resorts, owing to the reluctance of the North Eastern Railway to operate Sunday services for fear of upsetting the church goers.

REDCAR
The Esplanade 1886

When this photograph was taken, cycling was in vogue; the tricycle had been introduced during the 1870s. Most had two large driving wheels with a stabilizing wheel at either the front or back, or in some cases, both. Some tricycles were made to seat two people, either side by side, or in tandem.

REDCAR
The Sands 1906

On the right, there appears to be one of the few musical urinals in the British Empire: a combined toilet and bandstand.

REDCAR, THE ESPLANADE 1886   18131

REDCAR, THE SANDS 1906   54447

REDCAR
The Sands 1886 18133
In 1869, Dr Oliver of Redcar, wrote that 'Redcar is adapted to
the debilitated class of invalids not only by reason of its
powerful tonic atmosphere and excellent bathing, but
because of the natural facilities offered by its extensive beach
for easy exercise and locomotion'.

REDCAR, HIGH STREET 1885 18134
Sixty years earlier the village had five inns and taverns, all of which took in paying guests; the Crown & Anchor, the Jolly Sailor, the Red Lion, The Ship, and the White Swan. Also, at least sixty residents offered lodgings to visitors.

REDCAR, HIGH STREET 1913 66389
Redcar was once the most northerly of the Yorkshire resorts and was famed for its horse racing. Of the meetings held between May and October, the July Redcar Race Week became the most important fixture. By this time the resort had three hotels recommended in Baedeker's Guide: the Coatham, the Red Lion, and the Swan.

REDCAR, NEWCOMEN STREET 1901 48000
The post office is on the right. In the 1820s, when Robert Walker was the postmaster, there was a collection and delivery every day during the bathing season. Once winter set in, postal services operated on Mondays, Wednesdays, Thursdays and Saturdays.

SALTBURN-BY-THE-SEA, FROM THE COASTGUARD PATH 1885 18104
The older part of the town is to the left, with the resort on the cliff in the background.

SALTBURN-BY-THE-SEA, PIER ENTRANCE 1913 66354
The cliff lift was built to connect the Promenade with the Lower Marine Promenade and the pier.

SALTBURN-BY-THE-SEA, THE BRIDGE c1885 18109
Hazelgrove, the valley between the two cliffs, was laid out to provide a picturesque walk from the shore to the western side of the town. Spanning the valley is the 140ft high Halfpenny Bridge, which proved a handy observation platform for those holidaymakers eager to look at the views.

ROSEBERRY TOPPING 1932 85338
Three miles south west of Saltburn is Roseberry Topping, which rises to 1,057ft above sea level. It is not the highest of the Cleveland Hills: Burton Head rises to 1,485 ft, but Roseberry is acknowledged as offering the finest views.

GUISBOROUGH
The Market Place 1907 58660

Guisborough is the ancient capital of Cleveland. It was here, during the reign of Elizabeth I, that the first alum works in England was opened. In May 1822, a spring was discovered about one mile to the south west, and Guisborough climbed aboard the spa town bandwagon. To the faithful, the spring was said to relieve rheumatism and bilious complaints and was an excellent diuretic.

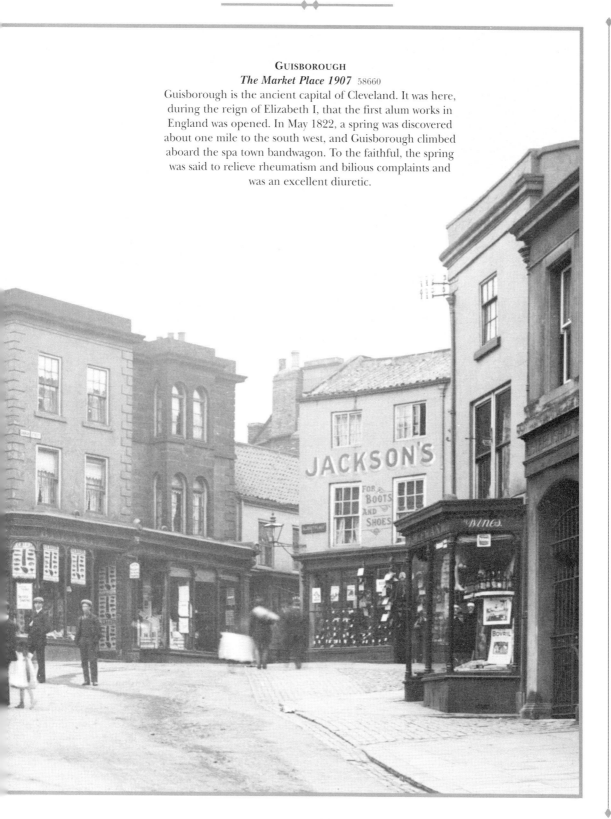

GUISBOROUGH, THE MARKET PLACE 1899 44756
In July 1740 a number of the inhabitants of Yarm were brought to the Guisborough Sessions, accused of riotous assembly. Will Artis was ordered to be taken hence to Whitby and 'thence on board some of his Majesty's shippes of warr'. Will's punishment was to be added to the press gang quota.

GUISBOROUGH, PRIORY AND LAKE 1932 85330
Founded around the year 1119 by Robert de Brus (Bruce), Second Lord of Skelton, Guisborough became very wealthy. The original building was destroyed by fire in 1289, but the Augustinian canons rebuilt on the grand scale. At the Dissolution the annual revenue of the Priory was £628 3s 4d.

GUISBOROUGH
The Priory 1885

The only remnants of the Priory now standing are a 12th-century gatehouse and the east end of the 14th century church. Near the Priory is the church of St Nicholas, which contains the Brus Cenotaph, on which are carved ten knights representing members of the family. Robert de Brus died at Guisborough in 1145.

◆

GUISBOROUGH
Highcliffe 1913

In 1748 cattle distemper was raging nationwide amid horned cattle. At Guisborough, an order was issued prohibiting the movement of all live cattle, even with a certificate. Farmers were compensated for losses, as the court ordered that Will Cass be paid 37s 6d for killing a cow suffering with distemper.

GUISBOROUGH, THE PRIORY 1885 18151

GUISBOROUGH, HIGHCLIFFE 1913 66020

STAITHES, CHURCH STREET 1925 79004
As with several other fishing villages along the Yorkshire coast, Staithes clings alpine-like to the sides of steep cliffs and ravines. Though the old man could be delivering milk, yokes were used for carrying all manner of things up the steep streets.

STAITHES, GENERAL VIEW 1886 18209
The village is said to have begun as the result of a shipwreck when survivors from a French ship scrambled ashore and decided to stay. During the 19th and early 20th centuries, Staithes was a fishing port of some standing, being a centre for cod, haddock and mackerel, with enough fish being landed for the North Eastern Railway to run three of four special fish-trains every week.

SANDSEND, EAST ROW 1925 78993
Sandsend is just three miles along the sandy beach from Whitby. It was a popular place for holidays, even though the village had been spoiled by the ruins of an alum works and an iron bridge that carried the railway line between Whitby and Saltburn.

SANDSEND, THE VILLAGE c1885 18190
A couple of miles to the north lies the tiny hamlet of Kettleness, or rather what is left of it. During a violent storm in 1829, the cliff fell into the sea, taking most of Kettleness with it.

WHITBY, GROUP OF FISHER CHILDREN 1891 28866
Situated in a deep ravine on the estuary of the River Esk, Whitby once earned its living from the sea, either by whaling, fishing, coastal trading or shipbuilding.

WHITBY, THE FISH QUAY 1923 74318

For some reason, fish quays seem to attract tourists and looking at this picture, things were no different in 1923. By the mid 18th century, Whitby was involved in whaling; blubber warehouses were erected along the inner harbour. Between 1766 and 1816, the Whitby fleet's catch included 2,761 whales and around 25,000 seals.

WHITBY, THE KHYBER PASS 1925 78977

The coming of the railway put Whitby on the tourist map; its harbourside streets, ruined abbey, and souvenirs made from jet, which is a fossilized wood found locally, all proved a magnet for holidaymakers. Holiday trade led to much of the development in the town, chiefly in the direction of the West Cliff, from which this photograph is taken.

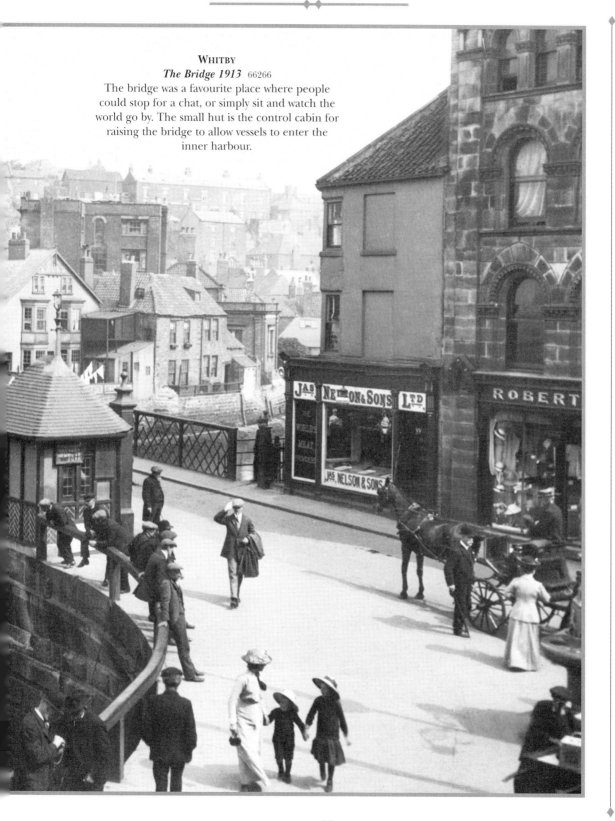

WHITBY
The Bridge 1913 66266
The bridge was a favourite place where people could stop for a chat, or simply sit and watch the world go by. The small hut is the control cabin for raising the bridge to allow vessels to enter the inner harbour.

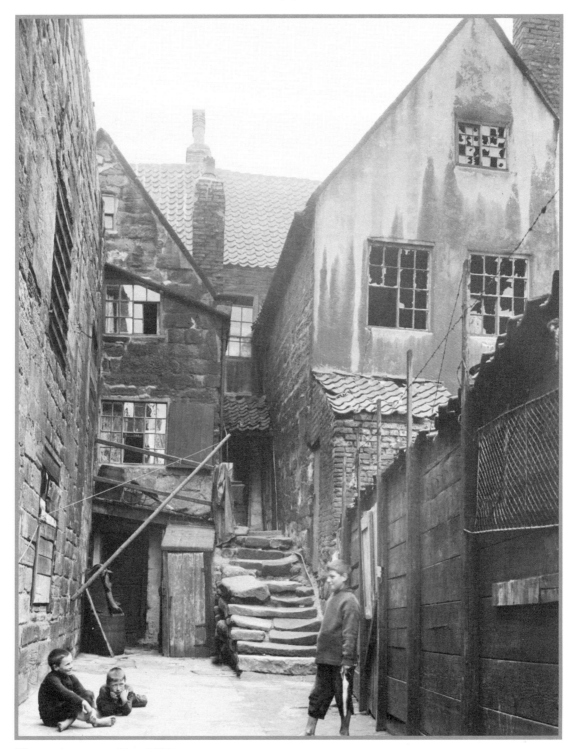

WHITBY, ARGUMENTS YARD 1913 66290
The house on the right appears derelict, and the stone stairs have seen better days. The outside toilet looks as though it could collapse at any minute, and does not appear to be the sort of place to get caught in.

WHITBY
Baxtergate 1923

A bustling, if somewhat winding, street. Along here were the post office, the Angel Hotel and St John's Church. By this date, Whitby had five hotels featured in the Dunlop Guide: the Angel, the Royal (with 172 beds and garaging for twenty automobiles), the Metropole, the Custom House, and the seventy-bed West Cliff.

◆

WHITBY
West Cliff 1901

The bridge has been raised to allow the passage of a small paddle steamer, which is probably on an excursion from Scarborough.

WHITBY, BAXTERGATE 1923 74309

WHITBY, WEST CLIFF 1901 46788

ROBIN HOOD'S BAY, GENERAL VIEW 1927 80183

Part of the village is clustered around the top of a ravine. Notice the steep steps in the lower foreground, dropping away toward the sea. The connection with the legend of Robin Hood is obscure, but one story is that he made his way here in order to hire boats in which to escape from England.

ROBIN HOOD'S BAY, FROM THE BEACH 1901 46795

It is low tide in this view looking towards the slipway and the Bay Hotel. The Bay itself sweeps around from Ness Point in the north to the 600ft high cliffs of Ravenscar, at the other end. Over the last two hundred years erosion has seen two rows of houses and a road crash into the sea.

ROBIN HOOD'S BAY, THE SHORE 1927 80187
For decades, just as in this picture, people have sun bathed along the sea wall. The place became a favourite with artists and holidaymakers alike; many of its red-roofed cottages were perched somewhat precariously on the cliffs. It is also known as Bay Town.

RAVENSCAR, FROM ROBIN HOOD'S BAY 1901 46803

Apparently there was once a plan to develop Ravenscar into a resort that would rival Scarborough, but the scheme failed owing to the unstable geology of the area. Ravenscar's name is said to be derived from Danish raiders who hoisted their standard here, on which was depicted a raven.

RAVENSCAR, THE RAVEN HALL HOTEL 1901 46805

The hotel stands on the site of Ravenshill Hall, which was built in 1774. It was during the construction of the Hall that a Roman inscription stone was discovered, commemorating the completion of a signal tower on the site in about AD400.

SCARBOROUGH, NORTH BAY 1891 28825

This photograph includes the pier and the castle. The castle was certainly being used in the 1870s by volunteer artillery units to conduct firing exercises and gunnery drills. One picture shows a battery comprising an odd assortment of pieces, including a Whitworth rifled field gun and two obsolete muzzle-loading 42-pounders: all in all, a supply officer's nightmare.

SCARBOROUGH, THE CASTLE 1890 23475

Here we see the approach across the narrow stone causeway which crossed the fosse. The keep was positioned in such a way as to command this entrance. Any attacking force attempting to enter the bailey was faced with the prospect of having to run the gauntlet of defending fire from the keep's battlements. The keep once stood 100ft high and has walls 12ft thick.

SCARBOROUGH
Castle Docks 1890 23468
The paddle steamers were used for excursion trips out
around the headland, as well as to Bridlington and
Whitby, and remained a feature of the resort until
replaced by screw vessels in the 1930s.

SCARBOROUGH, FISHING BOATS 1890 23467

In 1823, Scarborough was home to no less than 59 master mariners and 56 registered ship owners. There were six ship builders and one boat builder. Local vessels such as the 'Aid', 'Moscow', 'Trimmer', 'Fallowden', 'Commerce', and the 'Free Briton' ran to London, Hull or Newcastle, though some of the services were not regular.

SCARBOROUGH, WESTBORO' 1891 28817

Westborough was one of the main thoroughfares linking the North Eastern Railway station and the town. On the right is Winebloom's Railway Hotel and Robinson's Cash Boot Stores; on the left is Graham's Adelphi Commercial Hotel.

SCARBOROUGH, THE SPA SALOON 1890 23450

Writing in the 17th century, Dr Witte claimed that Scarborough water was a cure for apoplexy, epilepsy, catalepsy and vertigo, and that it cleansed the stomach, opened the lungs, and cured asthma, black and yellow jaundice, and scurvy. In all, it was a 'Most Sovereign remedy against Hypochondriack Melancholy and Windness'.

SCARBOROUGH, FORESHORE ROAD 1890 23464

Here, we see the market where trippers could buy fish caught by local boats. On the right is the lifeboat station, with the lifeboat slung on a wheeled cradle that could be hauled into the water, enabling the boat to float off.

SCARBOROUGH
Belmont 1890 23476
A family group takes the opportunity to admire the view over the Spa Cliff, or catch up with the latest news. The spa, by this time, was long gone, having been destroyed by fire in 1876. In its place an exotic Turkish pavilion was built containing a concert hall, art gallery, theatre and restaurant.

SCARBOROUGH, THE SPA PROMENADE 1890 23453

This was one of the town's main attractions. In the far background is the imposing bulk of the 300-bed Grand Hotel, which was designed by Thomas Verity and opened in 1867.

SCARBOROUGH, SOUTH BAY 1891 28809

The bathing machines are doing good business. In the 1720s, it was the custom for those 'taking the waters' to bathe in the sea. Gentleman were taken out into the bay in a small boat, or cobble, where they jumped stark naked into the sea. Ladies were obliged to bathe nearer to the beach, and wore some sort of gown.

SCARBOROUGH, THE SANDS FROM SPA GARDENS 1890 23459
The South Cliff Tramway offered an alternative means of escape from the beach to the Esplanade; the other way up was by the 224 steps cutting through the Spa Gardens. The tramway runs up the face of the cliff on a gradient of about one in three, and terminates opposite Prince of Wales Terrace. Thanks to the terrain at Scarborough, two other tramways were built; one near the Grand Hotel and another at St Nicholas Gardens.

FILEY

The Promenade 1897 39343

On the right Archibald Ramsden's bathing machines
offer discreet changing facilities for those ladies wishing
to take an invigorating plunge into the North Sea. The
small horse-drawn carts carried less active
holidaymakers onto the sands, but could also be hired
as an alternative to a donkey ride.

FILEY, THE SANDS 1897 39345
Judging by the crowd gathering on the beach, it looks as though a seaside concert party will shortly be giving a performance. Pierrot troupes were popular from the early 1890s, almost up to the outbreak of the Second World War. They dressed in clown-like costumes and their show consisted of songs, jokes and monologues.

FILEY, THE BRIG 1890 23488
The spectacular rock formation of Filey Brigg at the north end of the bay.

FILEY, THE SANDS 1927 80163
A hard way to make a living at this time was ferrying holidaymakers to and from pleasure boats out in the bay. Over at Blackpool, they used long mobile gangways at low tide and horse-drawn boat carts the rest of the time.

GOATHLAND
Beck Hole 1959
This lies between Goathland and Grosmont. It is noted for its woodland glens and the winding Murk Esk.

◆

GOATHLAND
The Village 1923
Sitting up on the moors, nine miles southwest of Whitby, is the village of Goathland. It became involved in the hydropathic movement with the opening of the Goathland Hydropathic Establishment. Such places offered guests various treatments using ordinary water, thus saving the visitor a trip to a spa town.

GOATHLAND, BECK HOLE 1959 G109023

GOATHLAND, THE VILLAGE 1923 74322

GOATHLAND, DARNHOLM 1953 G109009

The shallow ford at Darnholm, a tiny hamlet just up the road from Goathland. For decades the place has been a favourite with those who like nothing better than to 'bimble around' by the waters edge.

PICKERING, THE MARKET PLACE 1959 P156169

The parish church of Saints Peter and Paul became famous in 1851 when the vicar discovered a series of early wall paintings hidden under whitewash. He considered them ridiculous and ordered them covered over again, but at least he did not order them destroyed. They were uncovered again in the 1870s, and though they are heavily restored, they give us an indication of how medieval churches must have looked.

PICKERING, GENERAL VIEW C1955 P156107

Pickering Castle lies to the north of the town and was founded by William the Conqueror, though the earliest ruins date from the 12th century. The ruins are substantial, and include the curtain wall, three towers, a shell keep standing on a motte, chapel and halls.

LASTINGHAM, THE VILLAGE C1955 L173015

Lastingham is fewer than seven miles northwest of Pickering. In AD654 St Cedd, the brother of St Chad, built a monastery here, where St Chad died of the yellow plague in AD664. The crypt of the present church is thought to occupy the site of an earlier structure where St Cedd's bones were laid to rest.

HUTTON-LE-HOLE, THE VILLAGE c1955 H222009

The village of Hutton-le-Hole lies about one mile west of Lastingham. It was once the home of John Richardson, a Quaker missionary to the American colonies and a friend of William Penn, founder of the state of Pennsylvania. The Quaker connection with the village was very strong and a Meeting House used to exist on the site, which was later occupied by Brookside Cottage.

KIRKBYMOORSIDE, THE MARKET PLACE 1951 K130007

The old Black Swan Inn is noted for its timber porch, which is dated 1634, though the George & Dragon, an old coaching inn, also has its origins in the 17th century.

KIRKBYMOORSIDE, TOWN CENTRE c1955 K130010
George Villiers, 2nd Duke of Buckingham and friend of Charles II, was brought to Kirbymoorside after falling from his horse whilst out hunting. He was taken to a house where he later died of his injuries; it is now known as Buckingham House.

KIRKBYMOORSIDE, HOWE END c1955 K130012
The only hint that the picture dates later than the 1930s is the National Health Service prescription notice on the top of Goodall's.

HELMSLEY, MARKET SQUARE c1955 H201052
Helmsley is considered to be one of the area's more attractive market towns. This is the Market Square, with All Saint's Church and the monument to Lord Feversham. During the Civil War, Helmsley Castle was held by the Royalists, but surrendered after being besieged by Sir Thomas Fairfax.

YORK, VIEW FROM THE WALLS 1907 58687
To the left of York's city wall stands the station opened by the North Eastern Railway in 1877. To the right of the wall is the original station, which was opened in 1841, and used by the Great North of England and the York & North Midland railways. The wall had to be breached and an arch built in order to allow the tracks to enter the city.

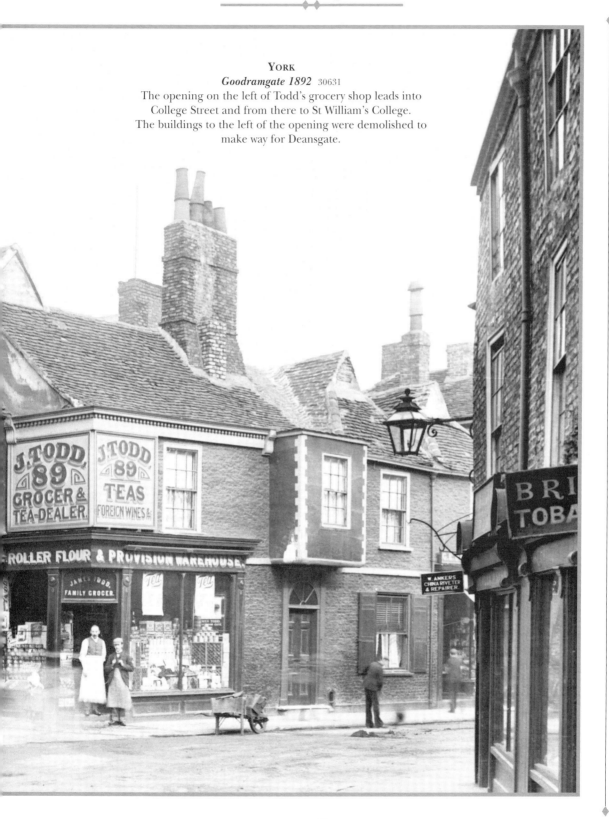

YORK
Goodramgate 1892 30631
The opening on the left of Todd's grocery shop leads into
College Street and from there to St William's College.
The buildings to the left of the opening were demolished to
make way for Deansgate.

YORK, MICKLEGATE BAR c1885 18440
It was here that the head of Richard Duke of York was displayed following the Battle of Wakefield. The last heads to be put on display were those of William Connolly and James Mayne, executed for their part in the Jacobite Rebellion of 1745-46.

YORK, THE GUILDHALL 1885 18460

The River Ouse flows past the embattled rear of the fifteenth century Guildhall, built in 1446. It was in this building that the celebration banquet marking the opening of the York & North Midland Railway was held, followed by a grand ball at the Mansion House. The building was bombed by the Luftwaffe in 1941, during one of the retaliatory raids for the RAF's destruction of the ancient city of Lubeck. It was restored to its former glory in the 1960s.

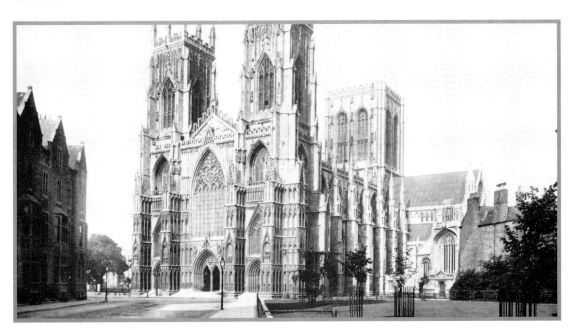

YORK, THE MINSTER 1891 28791

Begun in 1225 and completed in 1472, York Minster is considered to be one of the finest cathedrals in all England. In July 1984, the Minster was struck by lightning, which set the south transept ablaze. Damage was severe, and the great Rose Window suffered thousands of cracks. The strike was seen by some as a sign that the Almighty was displeased with the views of the recently enthroned Bishop of Durham's questioning of the virgin birth and resurrection.

YORK
Petergate 1892 30632
On the right are the premises of George Merriman, pawnbroker and jeweller. To the left is Searle's brush and mat warehouse. The large broom hanging over the doorway is now in the Castle Museum.

YORK, THE SHAMBLES 1893 32043

YORK
The Shambles 1893
The overhanging storeys were a feature of town architecture, which came into use some time in the late 13th or early 14th centuries. The Shambles were where the butchers had their shops, with open counters on which to display meat and hooks from which to hang joints.

◆

YORK
The Castle from Castle Mill Bridge 1885
The walls and towers surrounding the county gaol, court house and Clifford's Tower were not medieval. They were in fact designed by Sydney Smith, Rector of Foston, and built in the 1820s. The view is taken from the coal wharf on the Foss Navigation.

YORK, THE CASTLE FROM CASTLE MILL BRIDGE 1885 18494

YORK, CONEY STREET 1909 61723
During the Edwardian era Coney Street was the place for fashionable shopping. Both the top-hatted coachman and the young man in the automobile were waiting for ladies who were on a lunch-time shopping expedition in a nearby dress shop.

YORK, THE STATION 1909 61850
The magnificent sweeping curve of the station at York, the railway city of the north. During excavations beneath the platforms, human remains from the Roman period were found.

SELBY
Market Place 1913 65561
This celebrated market town is set on the Great North Road, and has one of the most magnificent abbey churches in England; the abbey was founded over 900 years ago by Benedict of Auxerre. Selby was once described as 'a cheerful-looking country town busied to some extent in flax-scutching, rope-making and boat-building'.

SELBY, THE OLD TOLL BRIDGE 1918 68170

Here we see the Ouse waterfront, with the abbey church rising over the roofs in the background. For centuries small boats journeyed up-river to unload at the town's dock.

TADCASTER, BRIDGE STREET 1907 58625

This bustling market town, dominated by lofty brewing chimneys, has been brewing beer since the 18th century. Here, on the left, is a fine old building, now a tea-room, with classic Hovis and Fry's signs tacked on to its frontage. Opposite are the bright new premises of Becketts Bank.

TADCASTER, VIEW FROM THE BRIDGE 1906 54849
Barges plied up and down the River Wharfe delivering to the breweries. In the distance is the 'Virgin Viaduct'. Built in 1849, it was never used - the railway that should have crossed it was never constructed.

WETHERBY, THE BRIDGE 1909 61726
Wetherby lies on the Great North Road and was once an important stopping point for coaches. In this picture, the River Wharfe flows placidly under the arches of the ancient bridge. A little further down, however, it surges over a weir where a watermill used to stand.

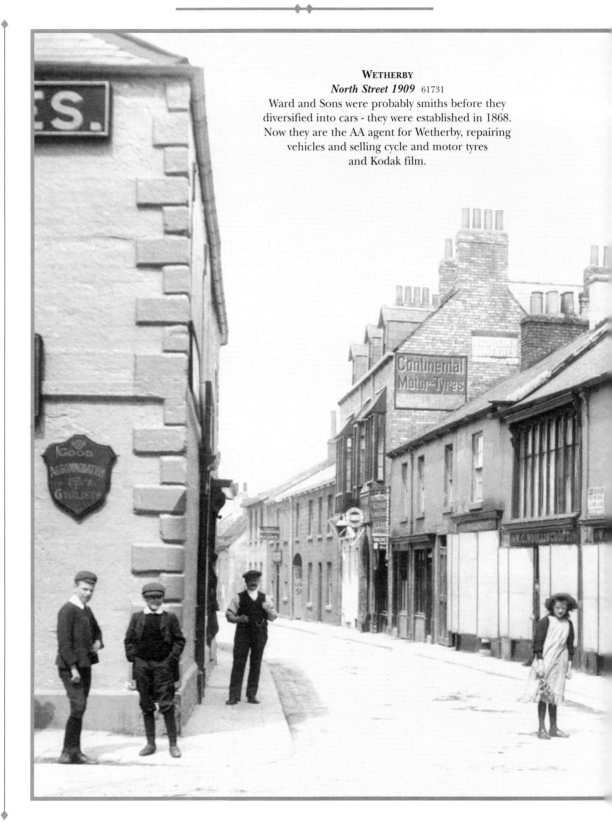

WETHERBY
North Street 1909 61731
Ward and Sons were probably smiths before they
diversified into cars - they were established in 1868.
Now they are the AA agent for Wetherby, repairing
vehicles and selling cycle and motor tyres
and Kodak film.

KNARESBOROUGH, THE TOWN AND THE RIVER 1888 20946

The church on the left is St John's and dates from the 13th and 14th centuries. The tower is topped off with a small spirelet, which can just be made out. In 1318 a Scots raiding party attempted to destroy the tower by setting fire to it. They failed, but for centuries afterwards the traces of the burning could still be seen.

KNARESBOROUGH, THE TOWN AND THE RIVER 1888 20944

In this picture we get a better view of St John's Church, which contains a monument to Sir William Slingsby, discoverer of the springs at Harrogate.

KNARESBOROUGH, THE CASTLE 1892 30611
Baron Serlo de Burg built the first castle at Knaresborough, and during the reign of King John the fortress was also a royal arsenal for the manufacture of crossbow quarrels. The castle was extensively rebuilt in the early years of Edward II's reign, after the lordship had been given to the King's favourite, Piers Gaveston. Richard II was held here, before being taken to Pontefract Castle where he was murdered.

KNARESBOROUGH
The Mother Shipton Inn 1914 67264
The Dropping Well is a petrifying well, similar to those
at Matlock Bath in Derbyshire, where the limestone content
of the spring water solidifies objects that fall into it.
At one time there was a petrified mongoose on display.

KNARESBOROUGH, THE OLD CHEMIST'S SHOP 1911 63543
Knaresborough boasts the oldest chemist's shop in England. When this picture was taken, a Mr Lawrence was the apothecary in charge, who ground his potions in a pestle and mortar.

KNARESBOROUGH, THE OLD CHEMIST'S SHOP 1914 67279
Inside the old chemist's shop. Note the pestles and mortars used for grinding up ingredients. Until 1840 some of this work was done in a large dog-powered pestle and mortar.

KNARESBOROUGH
The Ferry to the Dropping Well 1911
Moored alongside the far bank is a floating tea room, which appears to be doing a brisk trade. The rowing boat in the foreground is, in fact, the ferry to the Dropping Well. On the hill above the town stands the ruin of Knaresborough Castle, destroyed by Parliament in 1648.

◆

KNARESBOROUGH
High Street 1921
It was from inns and taverns along here that coaches used to arrive and depart. From the Bay Horse there was a coach to Selby; from the Elephant & Castle there was one to Thirsk, Leeds, York and Harrogate. From the Black Swan, a wagon ran every Monday, Wednesday and Friday to York.

KNARESBOROUGH, THE FERRY TO THE DROPPING WELL 1911   63532

KNARESBOROUGH, HIGH STREET 1921   71682

RIPLEY, THE MARKET CROSS 1923 74585
Ripley lies a few miles to the north of Knaresborough. The parish church dates from the 14th century, but was rebuilt in the 1820s. In the churchyard is what is claimed to be the only weeping cross in Yorkshire, and around the base are eight niches in which sinners may kneel and seek repentance.

RIPLEY, STREET SCENE 1923 74582
Oliver Cromwell once came to spend the night at Ripley Castle, home of Sir William and Lady Ingilby. Sir William was absent, but Lady Ingilby did not hesitate to tell the general that she would not admit him. Lady Ingilby was eventually persuaded to let Cromwell in, though when she met him at the lodge gate she was wearing a pair of pistols. The next morning as he prepared to depart, Lady Ingilby made it perfectly plain that had Cromwell not behaved peaceably he would not have been leaving the house alive.

HARROGATE, THE ROYAL PUMP ROOM 1907 58650
Here, bumpers of sulphuric and chalybeate water were dispensed from seven o'clock in the morning, after which a constitutional in the Valley Gardens was highly recommended.

HARROGATE
Valley Gardens 1907 58645
This was a favourite place for a mild constitutional
after taking the waters. Here a small crowd enjoys
an afternoon concert given by a Pierrot troupe.

HARROGATE, THE NEW BATHS 1897 39430
The Royal Baths first opened in 1897. When built, these baths were said to be unequalled in decoration and roominess. For 5s 6d it was possible to enjoy a 'mud bath' with electricity. From 1949, the cure was available on the NHS.

HARROGATE, PARLIAMENT STREET 1923 74570
A policeman directs the traffic. On the right are the Royal Baths, which cost nearly £100,000 to build; even the Kursaal, which opened in 1903, cost over £70,000. The money lavished on providing Harrogate with the best spa facilities in the country ensured that the town remained the most fashionable of all the spas for fifty years.

HARROGATE, THE STRAY 1902 48967
The stagecoaches are probably being used on excursions. In the background the buildings are Montpelier Parade (left), Cambridge Crescent (centre), and the Prospect Hotel which opened in 1859, but was enlarged in 1870. At this time, a room at the Prospect cost from 4s 6d per day; dinner cost 6s.

HARROGATE, PROSPECT PLACE 1911 63512
Most of the large hotels faced the Stray, including the Queen, the Granby, the Prince of Wales and the slightly smaller Empress. Harrogate also had its complement of hydropathic establishments including the Harrogate, the Cairn, the Harlow Manor and the Imperial Spa. Terms at hydros were usually at pension rates (room, meals, and services) and were around 63s a week, with water treatments extra.

HARROGATE
View from the Prospect Hotel 1902
A room at the Prospect cost from 4s 6d, with dinner at 6s a head, which put it in the same price as the Grand in Cornwall Road, but more expensive than the West Park, where rooms were from 3s, and dinner from 3s 6d.

HARROGATE
Parliament Street 1907
Two rival chemist's shops - on the right, Taylor's Drug Store boldly displays its name in six feet high gilt lettering. Not to be outdone, the chemist directly across the street proclaims that his establishment is the largest in the world.

HARROGATE, VIEW FROM THE PROSPECT HOTEL 1902 48970

HARROGATE, PARLIAMENT STREET 1907 58649

SKIPTON, THE CASTLE 1888 20955

The gatehouse of Skipton Castle, with its twin turrets. During the Civil War the castle was held for the King; it withstood a three-year siege before surrendering in December 1645 when stores and ammunition were all but exhausted.

SKIPTON, SWADFORD STREET 1923 74507

By now the motorcar and charabanc had put Skipton firmly on the map as the principal southern gateway to the Dales. The town boasted one RAC listed and two AA recommended hotels: The Ship, the Black Horse, and The Devonshire.

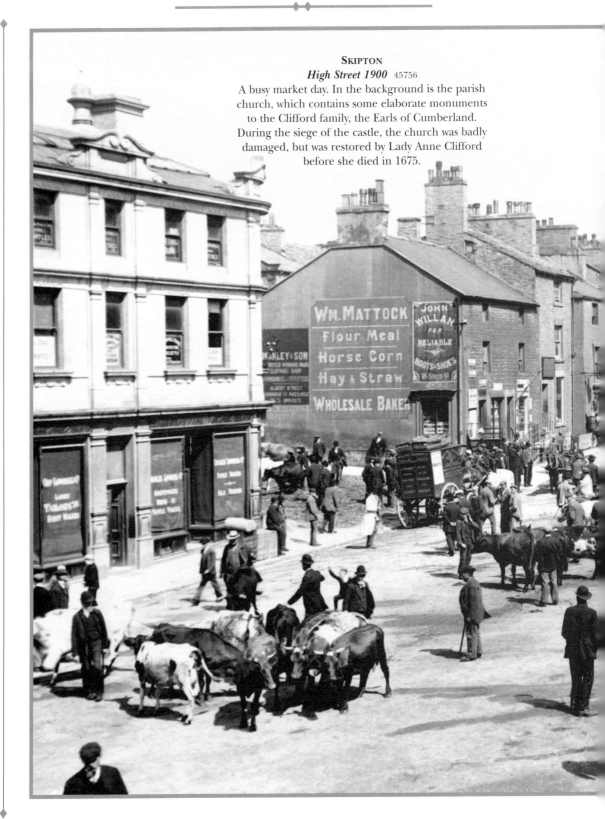

SKIPTON
High Street 1900 45756
A busy market day. In the background is the parish church, which contains some elaborate monuments to the Clifford family, the Earls of Cumberland. During the siege of the castle, the church was badly damaged, but was restored by Lady Anne Clifford before she died in 1675.

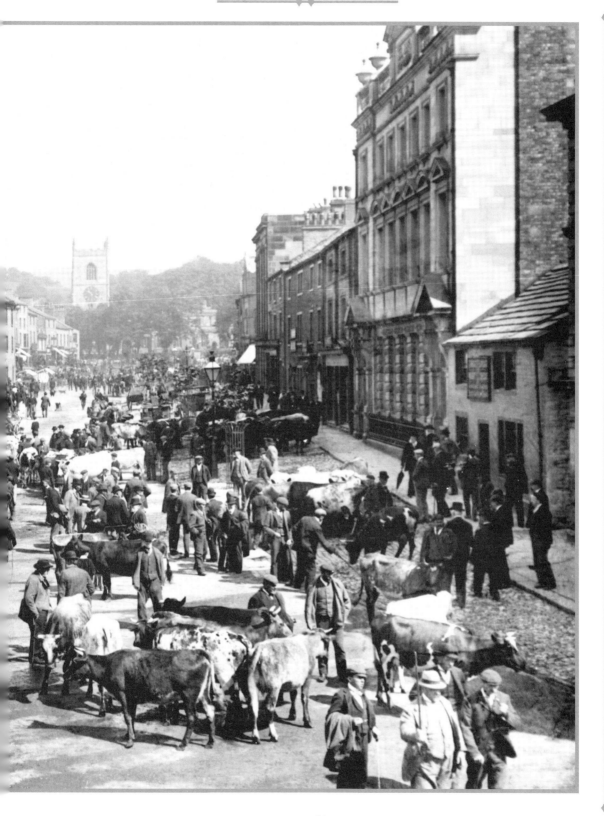

SKIPTON, STATION ROAD 1923 74511
The imposing main block of Dewhurst's Mill. By the 1830s there were 44 cotton mills in the Craven district, the main centres being Skipton, Settle and Barnoldswick.

BOLTON ABBEY, THE DEVONSHIRE ARMS HOTEL 1909 61883
This hotel at Bolton Bridge is less than a mile from Bolton Abbey. At this time the 40-bed hotel was already a favourite with motorists, though the hotel had carriages for hire for guests arriving by train.

BOLTON ABBEY, GENERAL VIEW 1921 71297
The majestic ruins are situated near a sweeping bend of the River Wharfe. The abbey has been a popular attraction for painters for many years, including Landseer and Turner. The priory was founded in the 12th century, and building continued right up to the Dissolution. The nave survived and was later used as the parish church; during the 19th century the refectory was used as a free school.

SETTLE
Market Day 1921 71339
Settle lies on the road between Skipton and
Ingleton. On the right is the Elizabethan-style
Town Hall, built in 1832, and in the background,
somewhat smothered by washing, is the Shambles.
Dating from the 17th century, the Shambles
comprised several shops in an arched arcade with
living accommodation over the top.

KETTLEWELL, THE VILLAGE 1900 45801

Situated in Upper Wharfedale on the road between Grassington and Aysgarth, the village was already a favourite with walkers when this photograph was taken.

GRASSINGTON, THE SQUARE 1900 45779

The village had once been a centre for lead-mining, but by 1900 it was once again reliant upon agriculture, though there was some quarrying in the locality. The railway finally came to the village in 1902 with the opening of a line to Skipton.

GRASSINGTON, THE RIVER 1926 79062
A quiet moment on the banks of the Wharfe.

BURNSALL, FROM THE SOUTH 1900 45793
In the distance is the parish church of St Wilfred's, which is noted for its Norse hog-back gravestones and a Norse font dating from the 11th century.

PATELEY BRIDGE, THE BRIDGE 1893 32022

Pateley Bridge, in Upper Nidderdale, lies on the road between Grassington and Ripon, and was once an important crossing point over the river. Before the bridge was built at least three causeways occupied the site.

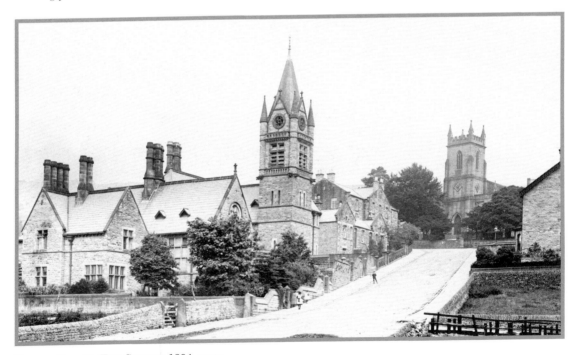

PATELEY BRIDGE, THE CHURCH 1894 32024

The old parish church of St Mary's dates from the 13th century, but was replaced by a new one, dedicated to St Cuthbert, in 1827. St Mary's still stands, but it is little more than a roofless ruin.

RIPON, WAKEMANS HOUSE 1924 75605

Situated in the southwest corner of the Market Place, the building dates from the 13th century and was the home of Hugh Ripley, the first mayor of Ripon, who was appointed in 1604. The Wakeman was the title of the chief magistrate of the town; Hugh Ripley was the last to hold the office under that title.

RIPON
The Market Place 1901 47179
The obelisk dates from 1781 and was erected to
commemorate William Aislabie, who was the local MP
for sixty years.

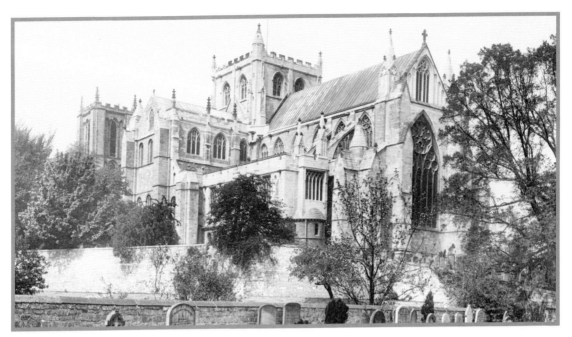

RIPON, THE CATHEDRAL 1895 35260
The cathedral looks massive, but is in fact relatively small, the central and two western towers being of no great height at all. The original church on the site was built by St Wilfred in the 7th century, but was destroyed in AD950. The present cathedral, with its fine west front, dates from the 12th and 13th centuries.

RIPON, THE MARKET PLACE 1914 67309
Every evening at 9pm, four blasts are sounded on a horn at the market cross. In days gone by, anyone whose house was robbed after the sounding of the horn could claim compensation off the Wakeman, if it could be proved that he had been negligent in his duties. The locals paid 2d annually towards the upkeep of the watch.

FOUNTAINS ABBEY 1886 3822

Founded in 1132, Fountains was given large tracts of land on which to raise sheep. A huge amount of English wool was sold abroad, often by means of forward contracts, which enabled the monks to spend money on ever more grand buildings. At one time Fountains had over 600,000 acres of land given over to wool production, but even so it was often in debt. In 1275 the abbey owed over £6,000 and was bailed out by the Jewish bankers in York.

BOROUGHBRIDGE
High Street 1907 58629
In 1322, the Earl of Lancaster sought refuge in the local
church following his defeat by Edward II. The unfortunate
Earl was taken prisoner and hauled off to his own castle at
Pontefract, where he was beheaded.

BOROUGHBRIDGE, THE BRIDGE 1907 58633
Boroughbridge, to the southeast of Ripon, dates back to Norman times, when a bridge was constructed over the Ure. It was then known as Burgbridge, the borough on the bridge.

BOROUGHBRIDGE, TOWN CENTRE 1907 58630
Boroughbridge probably saw its best days when it was a coaching town for traffic on the Great North Road and had no less than twenty-two inns. This picture shows the 14-bed Three Greyhounds Hotel.

MIDDLEHAM
The Castle 1893

A stone keep was added in 1170, followed by curtain walls and improved living accommodation. The castle passed into the hands of the Neville family, and in 1471 Richard, Duke of Gloucester, came here to be tutored by the Earl of Warwick. Richard later married the Earl's daughter, Anne, and their only son, Edward, was born here in 1473. Richard was killed at Bosworth in 1485.

◆

MIDDLEHAM
The Market Place and Cross 1908

The village church is dedicated to St Mary and St Alkelda, and owes its collegiate status to Richard III. Charles Kingsley was once an honorary canon here and wrote that Middleham 'is quite a racing town. Jockeys and grooms crowd the streets'.

MIDDLEHAM, THE CASTLE 1893 33130

MIDDLEHAM, THE MARKET PLACE AND CROSS 1908 59537

LEYBURN

The Market Place 1889 21690

The church looks six hundred years old, but was only built in 1836. Leyburn developed into a market town thanks to a charter granted by Charles I, but unlike Hawes and Askrigg, it never became industrialized. It proved to be a popular place for Yorkshire business people to retire, and the population doubled during the early years of Victoria's reign. The village was wealthy enough to support a theatre.

LEYBURN, THE MARKET PLACE 1934 86152
In the far left background is the Bolton Arms Hotel, a fine Georgian building complete with a Long Room where the Leyburn Market Club holds its dinners. In the market place is an iron ring, said to date back to the days of bull-baiting.

AYSGARTH, THE VILLAGE 1908 60790

The village owes its fame to Aysgarth Force, which comprises three main waterfalls, and a number of cascades. The upper falls can still be viewed from a 16th century single-arch bridge over the Ure.

AYSGARTH, THE FALLS 1889 21668

A part of the Aysgarth Force. On the left is the parish church of St Andrew, which, though medieval in origin, was rebuilt in the 19th century. It does, however, contain two carved screens, and a reading desk thought to come from Jervaulx Abbey.

ASKRIGG, THE POST OFFICE 1911 63469

The staff of Askrigg post office pose for the cameraman. Many of the buildings along the main street are imposing, three-storey houses, dating from the period when the town was a centre for lead-mining, cotton and worsted manufacture. Only the ordinary workers lived in nearby dilapidated cottages.

ASKRIGG, THE RIVER URE 1924 75699

Askrigg was already prosperous when the Domesday Book was being compiled. The town continued as the leading industrial and commercial centre for Upper Wensleydale until 1699, when Hawes was granted a market charter. From then on, Askrigg went into decline.

BAINBRIDGE
The Falls 1909

The River Bain flows out of Semerwater, the largest lake in the old North Riding, and into the Ure. At around three miles in length, the Bain is the shortest river in England. An annual custom is the blowing of a forest horn every night from September to Shrove Tide.

◆

HAWES
Market Day 1908

Granted a market charter by William III, Hawes later became a centre for textiles, quarrying and the production of Wensleydale cheese. The outdoor market is still held on a Tuesday, though a Market Hall was opened in 1902. In 1887, an auction mart was established for the sale of livestock; before this, auctions were held in the main street.

BAINBRIDGE, THE FALLS 1909   61768

HAWES, MARKET DAY 1908   60795

HAWES, THE MARKET PLACE 1924 75755
Motor vehicles dominate the scene in this market day picture, and at least one trader has crossed over the border into Lancashire to sell his wares.

HAWES, HAYMAKING 1924 75754

Mechanization might well have reached market traders, but down on the farm things were different. Here a sled is being put to good use during haymaking near Hawes. The parish church of St Margaret was rebuilt in the mid 19th century at a cost of around £3,000, having originally been erected in the late 15th century.

INGLETON, THE SQUARE 1929 82711

Just six years earlier than the date of this photograph, White Scar Cave, just off the road between Hawes and Ingleton, was discovered. With two waterfalls and coloured stalagmites and stalactites, the cave was an instant success with tourists.

INGLETON, THE VILLAGE 1890 26330

Ingleton is set amid the spectacular scenery of the River Greta and Clapham Beck. Francis Frith already has a stockist to sell his postcards. Until 1894, they had to be placed inside an envelope before they could be posted. Then things changed, and they could be posted without an envelope for half the normal rate. However, it was still forbidden to write anything on them save the recipient's name and address.

BEDALE, HIGH STREET AND CROSS 1908 59518

In the early 19th century the town had a population of around 1,100. The poor were reasonably well cared for. There was a hospital for six poor men of the parish, which had been founded in 1698, and a similar institution for three poor widows was founded by Richard and Thomas Young.

RICHMOND, THE MARKET PLACE 1908 59492

Holy Trinity church is a most unusual building in that a number of shops are built in it. In the 1900s these included a tobacconist's, a bank, and two butcher's. It now houses the regimental museum of the Green Howards.

RICHMOND, THE CASTLE AND THE BRIDGE 1923 74350

The Norman castle was begun by Alan Rufus in 1071 and dominates the entrance to Swaledale. In those days this was frontier country, for though William the Conqueror had won at Hastings, anti-Norman feelings in the North were high and the possibility of a Danish-backed rebellion was never far away.

Index

Frith Book Co Titles

www.francisfrith.co.uk

The Frith Book Company publishes over 100 new titles each year. A selection of those currently available are listed below. For latest catalogue please contact Frith Book Co.

Town Books 96 pages, approx 100 photos. County and Themed Books 128 pages, approx 150 photos (unless specified). All titles hardback laminated case and jacket except those indicated pb (paperback)

Title	ISBN	Price	Title	ISBN	Price
Amersham, Chesham & Rickmansworth (pb)	1-85937-340-2	£9.99	Derby (pb)	1-85937-367-4	£9.99
			Derbyshire (pb)	1-85937-196-5	£9.99
Ancient Monuments & Stone Circles	1-85937-143-4	£17.99	Devon (pb)	1-85937-297-x	£9.99
Aylesbury (pb)	1-85937-227-9	£9.99	Dorset (pb)	1-85937-269-4	£9.99
Bakewell	1-85937-113-2	£12.99	Dorset Churches	1-85937-172-8	£17.99
Barnstaple (pb)	1-85937-300-3	£9.99	Dorset Coast (pb)	1-85937-299-6	£9.99
Bath (pb)	1-85937419-0	£9.99	Dorset Living Memories	1-85937-210-4	£14.99
Bedford (pb)	1-85937-205-8	£9.99	Down the Severn	1-85937-118-3	£14.99
Berkshire (pb)	1-85937-191-4	£9.99	Down the Thames (pb)	1-85937-278-3	£9.99
Berkshire Churches	1-85937-170-1	£17.99	Down the Trent	1-85937-311-9	£14.99
Blackpool (pb)	1-85937-382-8	£9.99	Dublin (pb)	1-85937-231-7	£9.99
Bognor Regis (pb)	1-85937-431-x	£9.99	East Anglia (pb)	1-85937-265-1	£9.99
Bournemouth	1-85937-067-5	£12.99	East London	1-85937-080-2	£14.99
Bradford (pb)	1-85937-204-x	£9.99	East Sussex	1-85937-130-2	£14.99
Brighton & Hove(pb)	1-85937-192-2	£8.99	Eastbourne	1-85937-061-6	£12.99
Bristol (pb)	1-85937-264-3	£9.99	Edinburgh (pb)	1-85937-193-0	£8.99
British Life A Century Ago (pb)	1-85937-213-9	£9.99	England in the 1880s	1-85937-331-3	£17.99
Buckinghamshire (pb)	1-85937-200-7	£9.99	English Castles (pb)	1-85937-434-4	£9.99
Camberley (pb)	1-85937-222-8	£9.99	English Country Houses	1-85937-161-2	£17.99
Cambridge (pb)	1-85937-422-0	£9.99	Essex (pb)	1-85937-270-8	£9.99
Cambridgeshire (pb)	1-85937-420-4	£9.99	Exeter	1-85937-126-4	£12.99
Canals & Waterways (pb)	1-85937-291-0	£9.99	Exmoor	1-85937-132-9	£14.99
Canterbury Cathedral (pb)	1-85937-179-5	£9.99	Falmouth	1-85937-066-7	£12.99
Cardiff (pb)	1-85937-093-4	£9.99	Folkestone (pb)	1-85937-124-8	£9.99
Carmarthenshire	1-85937-216-3	£14.99	Glasgow (pb)	1-85937-190-6	£9.99
Chelmsford (pb)	1-85937-310-0	£9.99	Gloucestershire	1-85937-102-7	£14.99
Cheltenham (pb)	1-85937-095-0	£9.99	Great Yarmouth (pb)	1-85937-426-3	£9.99
Cheshire (pb)	1-85937-271-6	£9.99	Greater Manchester (pb)	1-85937-266-x	£9.99
Chester	1-85937-090-x	£12.99	Guildford (pb)	1-85937-410-7	£9.99
Chesterfield	1-85937-378-x	£9.99	Hampshire (pb)	1-85937-279-1	£9.99
Chichester (pb)	1-85937-228-7	£9.99	Hampshire Churches (pb)	1-85937-207-4	£9.99
Colchester (pb)	1-85937-188-4	£8.99	Harrogate	1-85937-423-9	£9.99
Cornish Coast	1-85937-163-9	£14.99	Hastings & Bexhill (pb)	1-85937-131-0	£9.99
Cornwall (pb)	1-85937-229-5	£9.99	Heart of Lancashire (pb)	1-85937-197-3	£9.99
Cornwall Living Memories	1-85937-248-1	£14.99	Helston (pb)	1-85937-214-7	£9.99
Cotswolds (pb)	1-85937-230-9	£9.99	Hereford (pb)	1-85937-175-2	£9.99
Cotswolds Living Memories	1-85937-255-4	£14.99	Herefordshire	1-85937-174-4	£14.99
County Durham	1-85937-123-x	£14.99	Hertfordshire (pb)	1-85937-247-3	£9.99
Croydon Living Memories	1-85937-162-0	£9.99	Horsham (pb)	1-85937-432-8	£9.99
Cumbria	1-85937-101-9	£14.99	Humberside	1-85937-215-5	£14.99
Dartmoor	1-85937-145-0	£14.99	Hythe, Romney Marsh & Ashford	1-85937-256-2	£9.99

Available from your local bookshop or from the publisher

Frith Book Co Titles (continued)

Title	ISBN	Price	Title	ISBN	Price
Ipswich (pb)	1-85937-424-7	£9.99	St Ives (pb)	1-85937415-8	£9.99
Ireland (pb)	1-85937-181-7	£9.99	Scotland (pb)	1-85937-182-5	£9.99
Isle of Man (pb)	1-85937-268-6	£9.99	Scottish Castles (pb)	1-85937-323-2	£9.99
Isles of Scilly	1-85937-136-1	£14.99	Sevenoaks & Tunbridge	1-85937-057-8	£12.99
Isle of Wight (pb)	1-85937-429-8	£9.99	Sheffield, South Yorks (pb)	1-85937-267-8	£9.99
Isle of Wight Living Memories	1-85937-304-6	£14.99	Shrewsbury (pb)	1-85937-325-9	£9.99
Kent (pb)	1-85937-189-2	£9.99	Shropshire (pb)	1-85937-326-7	£9.99
Kent Living Memories	1-85937-125-6	£14.99	Somerset	1-85937-153-1	£14.99
Lake District (pb)	1-85937-275-9	£9.99	South Devon Coast	1-85937-107-8	£14.99
Lancaster, Morecambe & Heysham (pb)	1-85937-233-3	£9.99	South Devon Living Memories	1-85937-168-x	£14.99
Leeds (pb)	1-85937-202-3	£9.99	South Hams	1-85937-220-1	£14.99
Leicester	1-85937-073-x	£12.99	Southampton (pb)	1-85937-427-1	£9.99
Leicestershire (pb)	1-85937-185-x	£9.99	Southport (pb)	1-85937-425-5	£9.99
Lincolnshire (pb)	1-85937-433-6	£9.99	Staffordshire	1-85937-047-0	£12.99
Liverpool & Merseyside (pb)	1-85937-234-1	£9.99	Stratford upon Avon	1-85937-098-5	£12.99
London (pb)	1-85937-183-3	£9.99	Suffolk (pb)	1-85937-221-x	£9.99
Ludlow (pb)	1-85937-176-0	£9.99	Suffolk Coast	1-85937-259-7	£14.99
Luton (pb)	1-85937-235-x	£9.99	Surrey (pb)	1-85937-240-6	£9.99
Maidstone	1-85937-056-x	£14.99	Sussex (pb)	1-85937-184-1	£9.99
Manchester (pb)	1-85937-198-1	£9.99	Swansea (pb)	1-85937-167-1	£9.99
Middlesex	1-85937-158-2	£14.99	Tees Valley & Cleveland	1-85937-211-2	£14.99
New Forest	1-85937-128-0	£14.99	Thanet (pb)	1-85937-116-7	£9.99
Newark (pb)	1-85937-366-6	£9.99	Tiverton (pb)	1-85937-178-7	£9.99
Newport, Wales (pb)	1-85937-258-9	£9.99	Torbay	1-85937-063-2	£12.99
Newquay (pb)	1-85937-421-2	£9.99	Truro	1-85937-147-7	£12.99
Norfolk (pb)	1-85937-195-7	£9.99	Victorian and Edwardian Cornwall	1-85937-252-x	£14.99
Norfolk Living Memories	1-85937-217-1	£14.99	Victorian & Edwardian Devon	1-85937-253-8	£14.99
Northamptonshire	1-85937-150-7	£14.99	Victorian & Edwardian Kent	1-85937-149-3	£14.99
Northumberland Tyne & Wear (pb)	1-85937-281-3	£9.99	Vic & Ed Maritime Album	1-85937-144-2	£17.99
North Devon Coast	1-85937-146-9	£14.99	Victorian and Edwardian Sussex	1-85937-157-4	£14.99
North Devon Living Memories	1-85937-261-9	£14.99	Victorian & Edwardian Yorkshire	1-85937-154-x	£14.99
North London	1-85937-206-6	£14.99	Victorian Seaside	1-85937-159-0	£17.99
North Wales (pb)	1-85937-298-8	£9.99	Villages of Devon (pb)	1-85937-293-7	£9.99
North Yorkshire (pb)	1-85937-236-8	£9.99	Villages of Kent (pb)	1-85937-294-5	£9.99
Norwich (pb)	1-85937-194-9	£8.99	Villages of Sussex (pb)	1-85937-295-3	£9.99
Nottingham (pb)	1-85937-324-0	£9.99	Warwickshire (pb)	1-85937-203-1	£9.99
Nottinghamshire (pb)	1-85937-187-6	£9.99	Welsh Castles (pb)	1-85937-322-4	£9.99
Oxford (pb)	1-85937-411-5	£9.99	West Midlands (pb)	1-85937-289-9	£9.99
Oxfordshire (pb)	1-85937-430-1	£9.99	West Sussex	1-85937-148-5	£14.99
Peak District (pb)	1-85937-280-5	£9.99	West Yorkshire (pb)	1-85937-201-5	£9.99
Penzance	1-85937-069-1	£12.99	Weymouth (pb)	1-85937-209-0	£9.99
Peterborough (pb)	1-85937-219-8	£9.99	Wiltshire (pb)	1-85937-277-5	£9.99
Piers	1-85937-237-6	£17.99	Wiltshire Churches (pb)	1-85937-171-x	£9.99
Plymouth	1-85937-119-1	£12.99	Wiltshire Living Memories	1-85937-245-7	£14.99
Poole & Sandbanks (pb)	1-85937-251-1	£9.99	Winchester (pb)	1-85937-428-x	£9.99
Preston (pb)	1-85937-212-0	£9.99	Windmills & Watermills	1-85937-242-2	£17.99
Reading (pb)	1-85937-238-4	£9.99	Worcester (pb)	1-85937-165-5	£9.99
Romford (pb)	1-85937-319-4	£9.99	Worcestershire	1-85937-152-3	£14.99
Salisbury (pb)	1-85937-239-2	£9.99	York (pb)	1-85937-199-x	£9.99
Scarborough (pb)	1-85937-379-8	£9.99	Yorkshire (pb)	1-85937-186-8	£9.99
St Albans (pb)	1-85937-341-0	£9.99	Yorkshire Living Memories	1-85937-166-3	£14.99

See Frith books on the internet www.francisfrith.co.uk

FRITH PRODUCTS & SERVICES

Francis Frith would doubtless be pleased to know that the pioneering publishing venture he started in 1860 still continues today. A hundred and forty years later, The Francis Frith Collection continues in the same innovative tradition and is now one of the foremost publishers of vintage photographs in the world. Some of the current activities include:

Interior Decoration

Today Frith's photographs can be seen framed and as giant wall murals in thousands of pubs, restaurants, hotels, banks, retail stores and other public buildings throughout the country. In every case they enhance the unique local atmosphere of the places they depict and provide reminders of gentler days in an increasingly busy and frenetic world.

Product Promotions

Frith products are used by many major companies to promote the sales of their own products or to reinforce their own history and heritage. Frith promotions have been used by Hovis bread, Courage beers, Scots Porage Oats, Colman's mustard, Cadbury's foods, Mellow Birds coffee, Dunhill pipe tobacco, Guinness, and Bulmer's Cider.

Genealogy and Family History

As the interest in family history and roots grows world-wide, more and more people are turning to Frith's photographs of Great Britain for images of the towns, villages and streets where their ancestors lived; and, of course, photographs of the churches and chapels where their ancestors were christened, married and buried are an essential part of every genealogy tree and family album.

Frith Products

All Frith photographs are available Framed or just as Mounted Prints and Posters (size 23 x 16 inches). These may be ordered from the address below. From time to time other products - Address Books, Calendars, Table Mats, etc - are available.

The Internet

Already twenty thousand Frith photographs can be viewed and purchased on the internet through the Frith websites and a myriad of partner sites.

For more detailed information on Frith companies and products, look at these sites:

www.francisfrith.co.uk
www.francisfrith.com
(for North American visitors)

See the complete list of Frith Books at:

www.francisfrith.co.uk

This web site is regularly updated with the latest list of publications from the Frith Book Company. If you wish to buy books relating to another part of the country that your local bookshop does not stock, you may purchase on-line.

For further information, trade, or author enquiries please contact us at the address below:
The Francis Frith Collection, Frith's Barn, Teffont, Salisbury, Wiltshire, England SP3 5QP.
Tel: +44 (0)1722 716 376 Fax: +44 (0)1722 716 881 Email: sales@francisfrith.co.uk

---

See Frith books on the internet www.francisfrith.co.uk

TO RECEIVE YOUR **FREE** MOUNTED PRINT

Mounted Print
Overall size 14 x 11 inches

Cut out this Voucher and return it with your remittance for £1.95 to cover postage and handling, to UK addresses. For overseas addresses please include £4.00 post and handling. Choose any photograph included in this book. Your SEPIA print will be A4 in size, and mounted in a cream mount with burgundy rule line, overall size 14 x 11 inches.

Order additional Mounted Prints at HALF PRICE (only £7.49 each*)

If there are further pictures you would like to order, possibly as gifts for friends and family, purchase them at half price (no additional postage and handling required).

Have your Mounted Prints framed*

For an additional £14.95 per print you can have your chosen Mounted Print framed in an elegant polished wood and gilt moulding, overall size 16 x 13 inches (no additional postage and handling required).

> *** IMPORTANT!**
> These special prices are only available if ordered using the original voucher on this page (no copies permitted) and at the same time as your free Mounted Print, for delivery to the same address

Frith Collectors' Guild

From time to time we publish a magazine of news and stories about Frith photographs and further special offers of Frith products. If you would like 12 months FREE membership, please return this form.

Send completed forms to:
The Francis Frith Collection, Frith's Barn, Teffont, Salisbury, Wiltshire SP3 5QP

Voucher for **FREE** and Reduced Price Frith Prints

Picture no.	Page number	Qty	Mounted @ £7.49	Framed + £14.95	Total Cost
		1	**Free of charge***	£	£
			£7.49	£	£
			£7.49	£	£
			£7.49	£	£
			£7.49	£	£
			£7.49	£	£

Please allow 28 days for delivery   *** Post & handling**   £1.95

Book Title . . . .   **Total Order Cost**   £

Please do not photocopy this voucher. Only the original is valid, so please cut it out and return it to us.

I enclose a cheque / postal order for £ . . . .
made payable to 'The Francis Frith Collection'
OR please debit my Mastercard / Visa / Switch / Amex card
(credit cards please on all overseas orders)

Number . . . .

Issue No(Switch only) . . . . .Valid from (Amex/Switch) . . . .

Expires . . . . Signature . . . .

Name Mr/Mrs/Ms . . . .

Address . . . .

. . . .

. . . . Postcode . . . .

Daytime Tel No . . . .   **VALID TO 31/12/05**

The Francis Frith Collectors' Guild

Please enrol me as a member for 12 months free of charge.

Name Mr/Mrs/Ms . . . .

Address . . . .

. . . .

. . . . Postcode . . . .

Would you like to find out more about Francis Frith?

We have recently recruited some entertaining speakers who are happy to visit local groups, clubs and societies to give an illustrated talk documenting Frith's travels and photographs. If you are a member of such a group and are interested in hosting a presentation, we would love to hear from you.

Our speakers bring with them a small selection of our local town and county books, together with sample prints. They are happy to take orders. A small proportion of the order value is donated to the group who have hosted the presentation. The talks are therefore an excellent way of fundraising for small groups and societies.

Can you help us with information about any of the Frith photographs in this book?

We are gradually compiling an historical record for each of the photographs in the Frith archive. It is always fascinating to find out the names of the people shown in the pictures, as well as insights into the shops, buildings and other features depicted.

If you recognize anyone in the photographs in this book, or if you have information not already included in the author's caption, do let us know. We would love to hear from you, and will try to publish it in future books or articles.

Our production team

Frith books are produced by a small dedicated team at offices in the converted Grade II listed 18th-century barn at Teffont near Salisbury, illustrated above. Most have worked with the Frith Collection for many years. All have in common one quality: they have a passion for the Frith Collection. The team is constantly expanding, but currently includes:

Jason Buck, John Buck, Douglas Burns, Heather Crisp, Isobel Hall, Rob Hames, Hazel Heaton, Peter Horne, James Kinnear, Tina Leary, Hannah Marsh, Eliza Sackett, Terence Sackett, Sandra Sanger, Shelley Tolcher, Susanna Walker, Clive Wathen and Jenny Wathen.